Spears were thrown with a woomera. Spear throwing had to hit the target.

Koon-i-ya is the word for a big snake. You run in a line like a snake.

'Bal-ga' is a hammer head shark. The game is kicking a ball to tag.

'Wu-ra' means a duck in Tasmania. This is a game with birds' eggs.

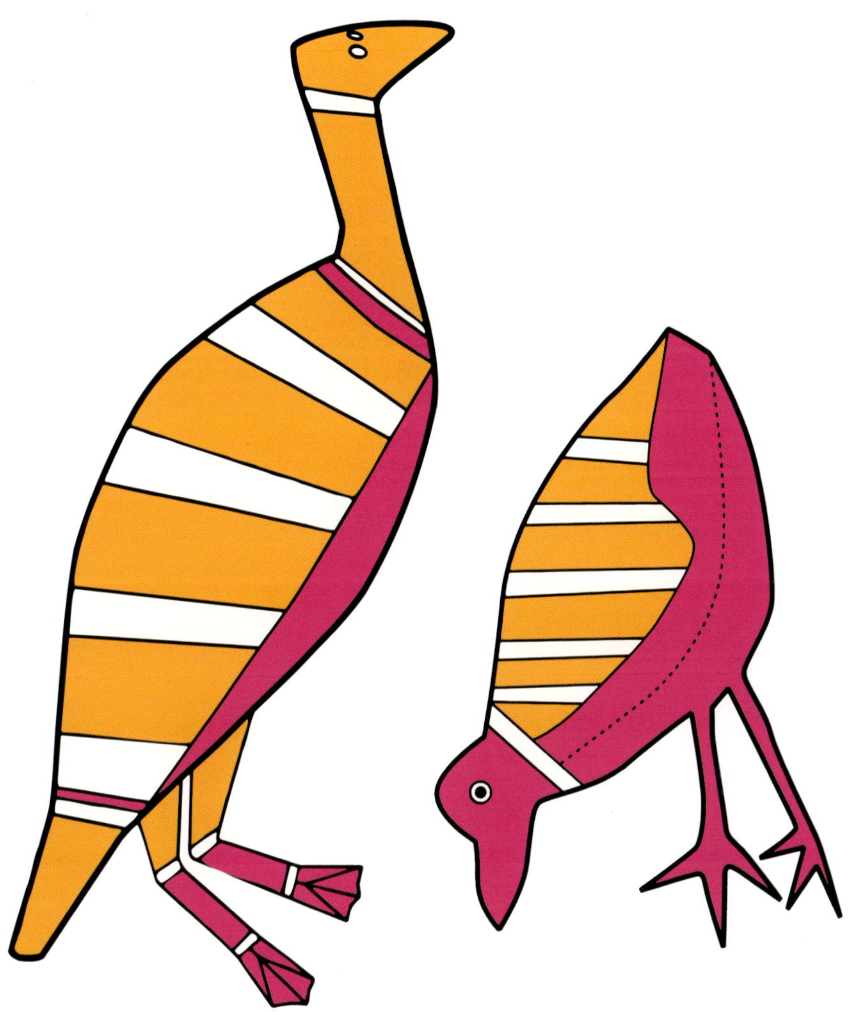

'Gi-id-jaa' are ants. This is a tracking game. This game looks in the sand for the ants.

'Ban-da' means a stone. This is a running game around stones.

'Yu-wan' is the word for snake to the Wik people. A rope game moving like a snake.

'Gib-ber' is a tagging game. This is a chasing game.

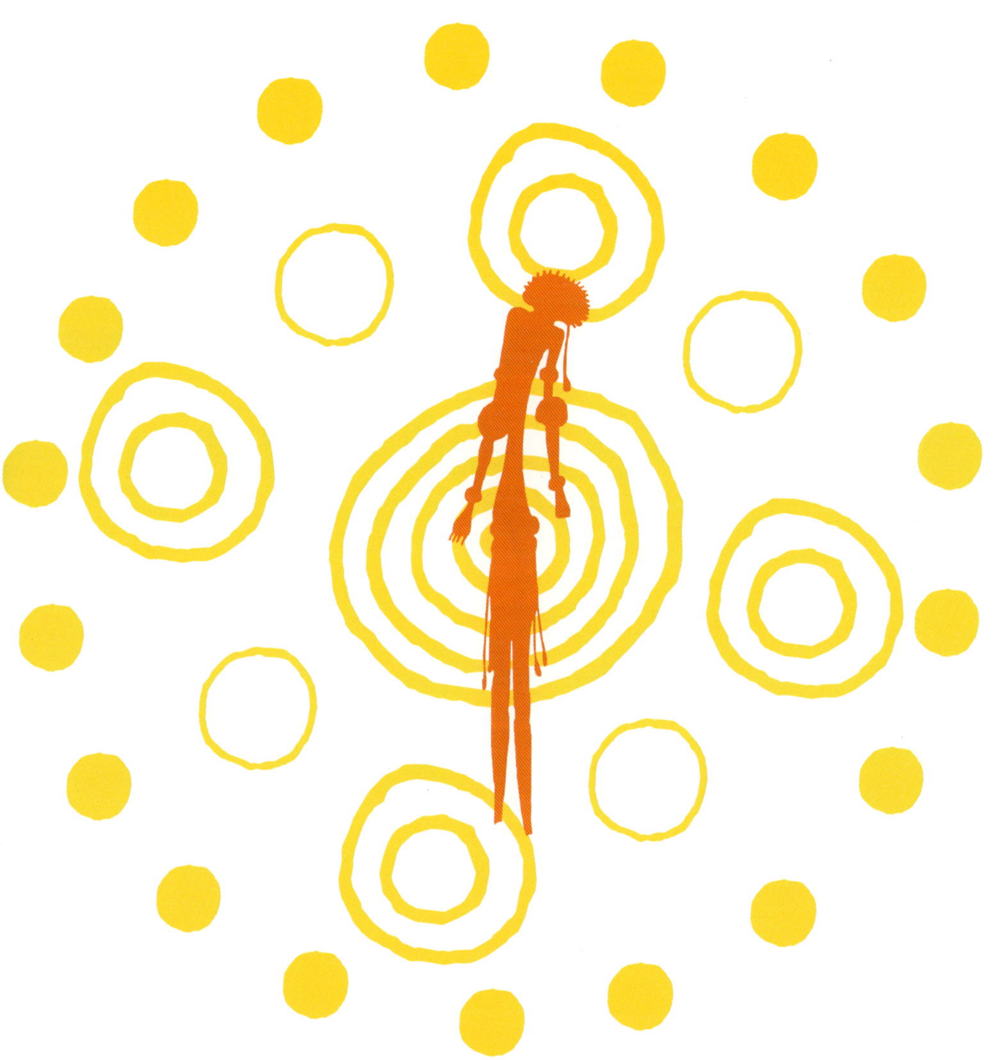

Children are playing spearing games. This was learning to hunt.

'Jim-ba' means star. Children can do star jumps with this game.

'Ba-ir-ba' means jumping. This is a game to make you strong. You jump to miss the spear.

Word bank

spears

woomera

thrown

target

snake

Tasmania

tracking

tagging

spearing

learning

children

jumping

strong